J-B
GIBB
455-0763

BOBBI GIBB, THE FIRST WOMAN TO RUN THE BOSTON MARATHON

WRITTEN BY Frances Poletti & Kristina Yee
ILLUSTRATED BY Susanna Chapman

Bobbi loved to run.

Into the woods, over the hills, through fields and by streams, Bobbi's feet flew across the earth. All of her friends ran and played too—until one day they stopped.

Bobbi missed her friends, but her legs would not be still.

Whenever she ran, the world seemed to disappear,
and only one sound filled her ears.

So she ran with her pack going higher and higher,
just her and the sound of the wind in the fire.

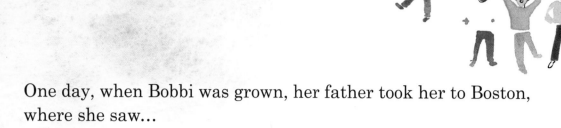

One day, when Bobbi was grown, her father took her to Boston,
where she saw...

Not a few, not a dozen, but hundreds of people, moving as one.
Kindred spirits, all running miles together.

Bobbi knew she had to be a part of it.

But her parents were afraid.

YOU'LL HURT YOURSELF!!!

GOOD GIRLS DON'T RUN

All Bobbi knew was that her legs wanted to move.

She went to the woods to think. "Can I run that far?" Bobbi asked herself, as her feet started pounding the ground. "I have to try!"

She ran further and further, and she ached and perspired,
and the world whooshed on by, like the wind in the fire.

So Bobbi left home with a secret plan. Away from her parents' disapproving eyes, she would train for the marathon. She traveled across the country, running in a new place every day.

She ran through lush forests in Ohio and Indiana, vast plains in Nebraska and Kansas, majestic mountains in Wyoming and Montana.

She ran with wild horses across sweeping valleys and stood on
Rocky Mountain peaks.

At night, she would set up camp and lie on the ground,
close to the earth, tired and happy.

She kept running every day, becoming stronger and stronger.
Then a letter arrived that made her stop in her tracks.

Her application for the marathon had been rejected.

WHAT if YOU injURE YOURSELF?

The rules are there for a reason

But Bobbi was determined to run.

She said she would do it, she wasn't a liar;
she'd show them by running like the wind in the fire.

She returned home and told her parents of her plans.
"Have you gone crazy?" cried her dad.

Bobbi knew he wouldn't be the only one to think so.
If she couldn't run as a woman, she would have to blend in with the men.

She bought a pair of men's running shoes—the only kind there was, since they didn't make them for girls. She borrowed her brother's Bermuda shorts and found a shapeless sweatshirt to wear over her black swimsuit.

As Bobbi pulled up the hood, her long hair was hidden and the disguise was complete.

Bobbi needed a ride to the starting line, but her dad refused.
He stormed out of the house, and everything was quiet.

She didn't know what to do.

There was a knock at Bobbi's bedroom door.
"Let's go," her mom said.

Bobbi's mom left her at the starting line. After running a few miles to warm up, Bobbi looked for a place to hide until the race started.

Her heart beat faster and faster. Would she be caught?

BANG!

The race had begun! She sprang from the bushes. Hundreds of feet were hitting the ground and Bobbi's were among them.

So she ran with the pack, going higher and higher,
the world whooshing by, like the wind in the fire.

Soon Bobbi heard murmurs. She'd been spotted! She nervously turned to look at the men running around her... but they were all smiles.

"Hey! Are you running the whole way?" one asked.

"I hope so!" said Bobbi—but she was getting hot. "I'm afraid I'll get thrown out if I take my sweatshirt off!"

The men replied, "We won't let anyone throw you out; it's a free road." They were on her side. Bobbi grinned, and she took it off.

Word spread quickly throughout the course.

A girl was running! They couldn't believe it!

The cheers were a roar. And Bobbi needed it. The ground was hard, her new shoes were stiff, and the final hill was still ahead.

But she couldn't stop now, though she ached and perspired,
and the world whooshed on by, like the wind in the fire.

Bobbi gritted her teeth as the road began to rise up before her. Closing her eyes, she imagined she was back in Montana running up the mountains, the soft earth under her feet.

Thirty steps,

then twenty,

Her throat burned from thirst and every step was agony
to her blistered feet.

It was time for the last push.

then ten...

Bobbi had done it! She was caught up in a whirlwind of reporters, radio presenters, and photographers.

History had been made…

Hearts and minds were forever changed.

The next day, Bobbi woke early; everything was quiet and still. Two days earlier the world had thought it was impossible for her to run a marathon. What else could be proven wrong?

Bobbi was looking forward to finding out. She put on her shoes and headed out into the woods, running again down familiar paths.

She ran with a strength only hope can inspire,
just her and the sound of the wind in the fire.

Bobbi Gibb

THE FIRST WOMAN TO RUN THE BOSTON MARATHON

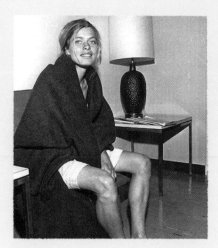

In 1966, Roberta "Bobbi" Gibb became the first woman to run the Boston Marathon. She did so after receiving a rejection letter from the Boston Athletic Association which informed her that women were incapable of running the marathon distance of 26.2 miles. At the time, the longest official U.S. race in which women were allowed to compete was 1.5 miles. People worried Bobbi would cause herself serious injury and thought that she was mentally ill. She finished the race ahead of about half the men who were running, with a time of 3:21:40.

Bobbi ran the marathon again in 1967 and 1968, joined each year by increasing numbers of women. In each of those years,

A woman, Kathrine Switzer, is given official numbers for the Boston Marathon in error. She runs, but is later disqualified. – 1967

Women are officially allowed to enter the Boston Marathon. – 1972

1896 – First modern marathon at the Athens Olympics.

1897 – First Boston Marathon.

1966–68 – Bobbi runs the marathon, joined by a steadily increasing number of women each year.

1972 – Title IX legislation is signed into law, prohibiting discrimination on the basis of sex in federally funded education programs, opening collegiate sports to an entire generation of women.

1975 – Boston Marathon becomes the first major marathon to include a wheelchair division.

Bobbi finished first among the women, leading to her being recognized by the Boston Athletic Association in 1996 as the pre-official women's winner for 1966, 1967, and 1968.

Bobbi went on to study philosophy and mathematics at the University of California, San Diego. She later conducted research at MIT while studying for her law degree. She has dedicated the latter years of her life to researching the causes of, and cures for, neurodegenerative diseases.

Bobbi divides her time between San Diego and Boston, where she writes, sculpts, paints, and of course, runs.

Bobbi runs the Boston Marathon for a fourth time. – 1986

Bobbi is recognized by the Boston Athletic Association as the pre-official women's winner in 1966, 1967, and 1968. – 1996

More than 12,000 women run the Boston Marathon every year. – TODAY

1984 – A women's marathon is added to the Olympics.

2001 – Bobbi runs the marathon again to raise money for ALS research.

2013 – Boston Marathon is the target of a tragic terrorist attack.

2016 – On the 50th anniversary of Bobbi's first run, Boston Marathon champion Atsede Baysa shares her trophy with Bobbi in celebration of the boundaries she broke for female runners.

WITH SPECIAL THANKS TO THE ENTIRE COMPENDIUM FAMILY.

CREDITS:

Written by: Frances Poletti & Kristina Yee
Illustrated by: Susanna Chapman
Edited by: Ruth Austin
Design & Art Direction by: Jessica Phoenix

Library of Congress Control Number: 2016957182
ISBN: 978-1-943200-47-4

2nd printing. Printed in China with soy inks. A021706002